How to Plan and Control Successfully ?

By

Chakrapani Srinivasa

How to Plan and Control Successfully?

By

Chakrapani Srinivasa

About the Author

Chakrapani Srinivasa (Padmaja), Freelance journalist from India possesses Bachelor degree in Engineering (B.E) and Post graduate in Business Management (MBA) with Distinction. He has worked as Associate Editor of 'Naradar' fortnightly journal in Chennai, India. He is the Senior Editor of the journal "The Divineness".

Contributed articles, short stories and travelogues in leading journals like Ananda Vikatan, Kumudam, Savi, Kalki, Dinamani Kadhir, Dinamani daily, Idhayam Pesukirathu, Naradar etc

He has written articles and e books through Smashwords Inc, Kindle Direct Publishing, Atlanta publications, Cooperjal publications (UK), lulu.com, ezinearticles.com, shvoong.com, iproclaim.com (USA) and TCC news (Germany).

He is the Consulting Editor: Contemporary Who's Who-Research Board of Advisors of ABI.

View his other books

Click to see my e books published by Amazon

http://www.amazon.com/s/ref=la_B01G3JTQ92_B01G3JT
Q92_sr?rh=i%3Abooks&field-
author=Chakrapani+Srinivasa&sort=relevance&ie=UTF8

#Pl visit my author's page in Amazon
https://www.amazon.com/-/e/B01G3JTQ92

Dedicated To My Dear Parents

Preface

Achievements of organizational objectives are made possible by planning.

The future role to be played and future programs to be chalked out, future expansion and so on are all under the umbrella of planning process.

This is under the rule of a manager.

On the basis of his career, experience, technical knowhow and the thorough analysis, planning is done for a prosperous future.

Contents

Process of Planning and Control

Scope for Planning

Achievements of organizational objectives are made possible by planning.

The future role to be played and future programs to be chalked out, future expansion and so on are all under the umbrella of planning process. This is under the rule of a manager. On the basis of his career, experience, technical knowhow and the thorough analysis, planning is done for a prosperous future.

Depending upon the post held by an individual, the scope of planning also varies. Lower the designation lesser area of coverage of his plans. Greater the level of post like the Chairman, the supremacy of plans extends to wider circle, even to international level.

With proper perception, establishment of targets, appraisal and exploration planning is executed meticulously. Strategic and operational planning covers long range planning and short range planning respectively. But this is only one side of a story for achieving the desired goal. Another magnificent phenomenon is 'control', which holds the vital key for all these plans.

Mere paper work and chalking out what to do and what not to do are not sufficient.

Proper Control

With utmost prudence, all the chalked out plans are to be executed with adequate 'control'. If only the 'control' exists, the prosperity and success of planning also exists and thrives.

Just like a hunter, who aims to kill a Lion and at the same time you have to select the right arrow and bow and trigger the arrow in the right direction, right speed and right angle to finish off the Lion you had aimed for or planned for.

This is a layman example to show how planning and control are interlinked for an execution of a work. Mere planning alone is not sufficient. Good control over the work, aiding the entire process will 'finish' the work commendably.

Panther Incident

In a recent incident in Cuddalore near Pondicherry, when a panther had entered a village, the villagers planned to capture it.

That was their aim.

But with a careful control over all their activities like following it amongst the bushes; watching on top of the tress, waiting with a goat in a cage, utilizing rain, which enabled the panther to enter for shelter they toiled sleeplessly day and night.

Finally the villagers obviously and fantastically captured that panthers, to occupy the headlines in the news paper.

Interlinked

Planning and control do have good interlinking aspects, which results in blossoming of organizational achievements with flying colors.

Control maintains standards, prevents deviations from plans, set rights the erroneous parts of actions, restricts the plans and reinforces perfection.

If our body is planning, then the heart, blood circulation etc are the controlling elements.

Controls are molded on plans. It forms the structure to discriminate between the areas, where they are accountable and non-accountable.

Levels

The controlling actions are according to the designation and levels of post in the organization. It should not exceed on decrease. A General Manager has control with larger scope than that of a Foreman.

On large scale and for longer period the controlling actions should be exercised. Controls should serve a strategic purpose.

Self Control

A control will be materialized only if the phenomenon is a tolerable one, by the subordinates. Or else an enormous amount of opposition will exists. All the plans will not be achieved if this intolerable action exists.

With lot of prudence controlling should be implemented as any negligence in this regard will fetch negative results.

Also periodicity of control has a say on the execution of plans.

Frequent monitoring and occasional controls are two segments of usage of control. Self control of an executive builds a right image for the organization and exemplary path to the subordinates.

Various Options

Management information, system external audits and budget preparation can be classified as periodic controls. PERT Charts, information passed on by others, special investigation and review reports are the occasional controls.

These controls are stepping foot path for leading towards successful planning operations.

Direct or indirect, formal or informal, centralization or delegation are the various options in implementing control.

Case Study-a PSU

In a popular PSU, this interlinking of planning and controlling was clearly visible at all levels.

Erection and installation of a huge multi crore project was a strategic plan formed by the management.

An increase in the Power Generation from 600 mw to 2070 mw due to this new project is nothing but a planning for the future need of the grid and future employment opportunities.

The demand of power has increased abundantly due to rise in domestic needs (due to rise in population) and industrial needs arising out of enormous growth of factories.

Anticipating the rise of need, the Ministry of Coal and Power were appraised by the PSU management with a plan for the erection of that project.

Facts and figures were submitted for this plan, by the CEO and Board of Directors.

This sort of planning for the long range of years is nothing but a strategic planning.

Submission of plan and report to the Delhi authorities alone is not sufficient.

The tool of 'control' was exercised at every stage scrupulously to see that our aim was fulfilled and succeeded.

Concurrence was obtained from Central Electrical Authority for the erection of this project.

A feasibility report from them is necessary for approval of the plan by the Central Government. They are the competent authority to say 'Yes'.

The environmental aspects had to be studied and any hazard to it will be considered as a negative point.

So, all the steps were taken to impress the Central Government that environmental safety will be adhered to.

The availability of fuel and water, which are the main source of raw materials for power generation, was put forth to the Delhi authorities.

Starting of Second Mine cut for lignite and the quantity of water pumped out from that basin were also put forth to the Delhi authorities.

The quantity of Lignite in terms of million tones, which can be utilized for 200 yrs and quality of the lignite in terms of calorific value, ash content, moisture were analyzed and submitted for concurrence.

Direct and indirect employment opportunities were mentioned with due calculation in the Executive cadre and Workmen cadre.

With an excellent perception, all the above planning was done and executed with control of Director (Power) through a 'New Project Office' formed under a General Manager.

Entire control was done through them, with due delegation of power.

After pleasing the CEA, Ministry of Coal & Power, the next stage they approached was the Finance Ministry for funds.

Without funds nothing is possible.

The plan may be useful and essential but financial control is in the hands of Finance Minister.

His team of men had to be convinced.

So, the entire calculation in the form of
- Investment (in crores) for machineries,
- Erection works,
- Commissioning works,
- Anticipated production of power in terms of million units,
- The price at which it will be sold,
- Return of revenue from the consumers etc,

      - should be given in black and white.

These aspects were submitted by the Director (Finance) under the team of Gen. Mgr (Finance), DGM, Chief Financial Controller etc.

So, delegation of work in this respect was done for better control over the work.

Thus the special reports for the future plan of the new project were prepared.

This comes under the occasional controls.

After getting approval from the Ministry of Finance, the entire plan has been safely concurred through the correct path of control.

Once the project approval was obtained from Delhi, action path was determined for execution of work at each level.

Action Path:

CEO:
- to appraise the Delhi authorities
- to negotiate with foreign consultants, erectors on collaboration matters
- To direct the Board of Directors in the field of Finance, Power, Mining etc.

- To feed back the erection progress to the Delhi Ministry level.
-

Board of Directors:

- to delegate the works to the Chief General Manager, General Manager in their field
- monitor through these immediate subordinates
- feed back to CEO

Chief General Manager:
- delegation of works to General Managers and other subordinates
- report to Director or CEO

So, in this respect the General Manager and other categories delegate the authority and have a direct control.

The bottom most level engineer in the floor will have indirect control.

Periodic Controls:

As the erection was under progress, the periodic control was implemented.

Progress details in the form of reports were submitted as the erection works were in progress.

The expenses were submitted by Chief financial controller of the project and they were audited by Controller of Audit General as ours is a Government concern.

The erection work was for a period of 3 to 4 years and hence budgets were prepared right from the erection up to commencement and after each year. Future allocation of funds and increase in budget were analyzed.

Occasional Control:

For erection work PERT charts were prepared. Right from the drawl of materials from the manufacturing factory till the erection of those materials to the desired place in the site, all details covering the responsibilities, time span and anticipated completion period were chalked out.

Since number of agencies were involved in this multi crore project, allocation of work, time slab for them, handing over time etc were fixed in the chart. So, following this chart the work schedule was perfectly controlled and coordinated.

Now the erection work was over.

Is this sufficient?

The objective for the management is to achieve the production and show the revenue, profit etc.

Output Control:

To get the desired output in the form of generation and profit this control has to be exercised. To conform to the planned output necessary control was exercised right from top level to bottom most workers. The required confidence was built in them. Incentives and targets were fixed and rewarded.

Employees were highly enthused to work more.

All motivational techniques were followed for up-keep of output control. Without this output the desired revenue cannot be achieved. What we had planned was obtained and it was shown to the Delhi authorities that every paisa invested had borne wonderful fruits for the benefit of entire nation.

Cultural Control:

The foundation for that PSU was laid by a renowned personality in India. His broad and immaculate vision of success had to be brought into reality. We have to strive for it exercising all possible controls on men and machines.

Selections of personnel's with dedication were done and due training programs abroad and within India were given to make the industry a strong fort of success. They were made to realize the importance of public money invested in that PSU.

All the dreams of our beloved founder were fulfilled and plans were materialized with zeal and effort.

For earmarking this success over plan and control, that project received the National Award for completing the erection and commissioning works in record time and an Award for Maximum Plant Load Factor amongst all PSUs with a record profit of Rs160 crores, exceeding all previous years' records.

With some special qualities, some individuals are identified from others.

So, also in an organization the disparity in the style of functioning gives a special tint to each management.

All the five fingers are not alike.

So also this phenomenon exists in the case of all organizations.

Corresponding to the mode of situations it has been framed and developed and still running on the track. This special feature can be termed as organizational culture.

There should be a fire for a smoke.

So also there will be a stimulus for any activity in that organization.

This stimulus is the determinant of organization culture.

In that PSU we have several determinants since it is a very large organization with multifarious activities and enormous man-power.

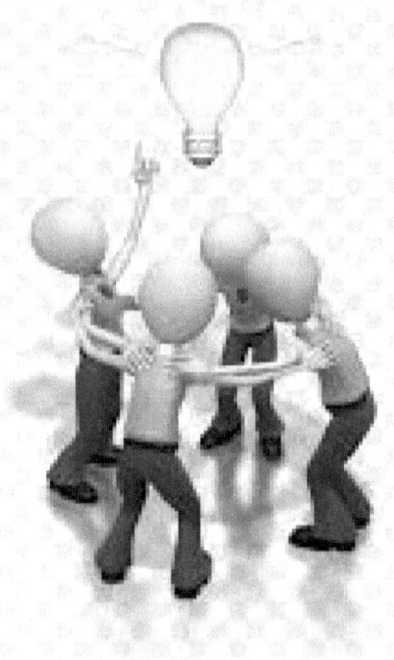

Economic Conditions

Our plant executive once approached the -ups in Finance and made a request that fund

has to be allocated for replacement of some equipments in the office rooms in the project.

The reply received from higher up was "Does that material gives any profit to the organization?"

That was the culture he had for spending.

He was a production oriented gentleman.

"I am prepare to shell out funds for machineries, which are essential for production"- he used to remark.

All our objectives are for production, which ensures profit.

Limitations are set for each officer category to spend. Hence a tight rope is tied to each officer and it is controlled by the reputed Director of Finance.

Even at the time of profit, that PSU will consider a program of expansion, re-investment, job opportunities, promotions etc.

When the Staff members approached the management for monetary benefits "Don't ask money like workers. Ask for perks and not money" was the reply from the management.

Even our CMD in one of his address to a large gathering said "I am not prepared to make any commitments or promises in the monetary side, as it has been cautioned by Director (Finance) that prior consultation and securitization are needed".

Such is the financial carefulness of our management and that's why that PSU is still proceeding towards profit, which is increasing year by year.

This strictness in issue of funds may cause resentment amongst the employees, but a sense of relief is seen when profits soar with increased incentives and other amenities.

Pay scales have been made at par with Coal India, which is a bold step taken by the management. It is all because of the care taken to allocate funds in the right spirit and in right direction.

The management is tight lipped to commitments and dealings with union people. These are done prudently and cautiously.

Funds for development of technology (even it is risky) are given due consideration. Introduction of computers, LAN, WAN V-SAT, etc are done at a rapid rate. AS400 computers are installed in Administrative office Computer Centre.

Life Extension Program (LEP) taken up by our management is an ideal step of economical maturity.

Many units are in service for the past 25 years.

There is a limit for efficiency of Boilers, Generators, Turbines etc concerned for power generator. Once a period of utilization had exceeded a limit, then it has to be replaced with a new one.

But that PSU suggested the Central Electrical Authority and Ministry of Coal and Power Government of India, that instead of going for a brand new one, the existing equipments can be replenished and taken for use. This will save several crores of rupees. This will extend the life of the plant for further 15 years trouble free.

The Government of India patted this PSU and gave a green signal for it. On that basis 2 units of First Thermal Station have given life extension and more than 300 crores of rupees were saved.

Now other two units also have given life extension program.

To improve the capacity and to meet the demand 2 more units of each 210 mw have been recommended and funds have been granted for it.

So for any expansion of the production and for job opportunity factors, funds are spent liberally.

A popular funding unit abroad granted loan for several crores for this expansion works.

Funds from the consumers are to be collected with promptness and judiciousness.

So, collection of revenue is also an imperative factor.

A certain amount of political pressure has to be experienced in this venture.

The financial personals in that PSU are well versed to face the anticipated crisis.

Our management has to depend on its own resources at one stage.

So the floating of Debentures and Equity Shares were done.

All the employees were offered 200 shares so as to form a participative management.

As a shareholder and as an employee all are proud to be under the shelter of that PSU, which has surpassed other PSU's in terms of financial achievements.

Good planning and control leads to growth.

Other books by the author

Strange India
https://www.amazon.co.uk/dp/B07S73LCTK

Waves of Wit on the Sea of Satire: Fun Butter Jam!!
https://www.amazon.co.uk/dp/B07XF5DT7 2
Kohlinoor of India: Winner Virat Kohli
https://www.amazon.co.uk/dp/B07SKNRVCT

Never Forgotten Naradar Srinivasa Rao: Most Enterprising Journalist
https://www.amazon.co.uk/dp/B07NLFY73C

How to Manage Funds in an Organization?
https://www.amazon.co.uk/dp/B00Z0Q8IF8

Wonders of Nano Technology
https://www.amazon.co.uk/dp/B07D3ZP7MC

How to become a Leader?
https://www.amazon.com/dp/B08BF4HCVX

What are the Best HRD Tactics?
https://www.amazon.co.uk/dp/B07HZ7JK18

Solar Energy Plans in Tamilnadu
https://www.amazon.co.uk/dp/B01G44ZL4K

How to Forecast Manpower Needs in an Organization: You Have The Skill!

https://www.amazon.co.uk/dp/B0111GBZKK

Infrastructure in India

https://www.amazon.co.uk/dp/B0163777RW

Accountant's Role in an Organization: A book for Accountants

https://www.amazon.co.uk/dp/B00YYHDHU0

Inland Waterways and Hydro Power in India

https://www.amazon.co.uk/dp/B015NEZMXW

Strategies in an Organization

https://www.amazon.co.uk/dp/B015AV1ZWU

How to Forecast Manpower Needs in an Organization: You Have The Skill!

https://www.amazon.co.uk/dp/B0111GBZKK

Infrastructure in India

https://www.amazon.co.uk/dp/B0163777RW

Accountant's Role in an Organization: A book for Accountants

https://www.amazon.co.uk/dp/B00YYHDHU0

Inland Waterways and Hydro Power in India

https://www.amazon.co.uk/dp/B015NEZMXW

Strategies in an Organization

https://www.amazon.co.uk/dp/B015AV1ZWU

Conflict Management Styles and Collective Bargaining

https://www.amazon.co.uk/dp/B00Z3B9GTW

Quiz and General Knowledge

https://www.amazon.co.uk/dp/B01N4M99S7
In Search of Paradise and Peace

https://www.amazon.co.uk/dp/B07C7F3XKM

Graphene -The God of Nano Technology

https://www.amazon.co.uk/dp/B07561LWTT

You Can Gain Power and Authority

https://www.amazon.co.uk/dp/B00YWY9QR8

HRD Systems and Management by Objectives

https://www.amazon.co.uk/dp/B016UC9UKC

International Conferences on Nanotechnology in India

https://www.amazon.co.uk/dp/B07BP8YLJZ

Holy Madhwa Saints: Get Divine Pleasure by Reading

https://www.amazon.co.uk/dp/B010WNBYU4

Trade Shows in India and Participants

https://www.amazon.co.uk/dp/B016PV1KS8

Collaboration and Intervention Techniques

https://www.amazon.co.uk/dp/B0110DLE8C

How to Plan Career and Quality Discipline in an Organization? Plan for Prosperity

https://www.amazon.co.uk/dp/B011GXOXIE

How to Become a Professional Manager? For You It Is Possible!

https://www.amazon.co.uk/dp/B011G4T6BM

Process of Planning and Control

https://www.amazon.co.uk/dp/B010ZHIBJE

How to Speak Skillfully?
https://www.amazon.com/dp/B08BJ8PCKT

How to Supervise Efficiently?

https://www.amazon.com/dp/B08BNFYSPQ- e book
https://www.amazon.com/dp/B08BR8YYG6?ref_=pe_3052080_397514860

How to Develop Systems for Profit?

https://www.amazon.com/dp/B08BYVL2P9

Nanotechnology Research in India

https://www.amazon.com/dp/B08BZDFVR8

How to Create a Turnaround in Your Organization?

https://www.amazon.com/dp/B08C97X2F9?ref_=pe_3052080_397514860

Click to see my e books published by Amazon

http://www.amazon.com/s/ref=la_B01G3JTQ92_B01G3JTQ92_sr?rh=i%3Abooks&field-author=Chakrapani+Srinivasa&sort=relevance&ie=UTF8